THE STRAYAWAY CHILD

A STORY OF GRIEF AND TRANSCENDENCE

ANNE GODAR HESS

I dedicate this book to my son, Will Hess,
and to the memory of my daughter, Kate Hess.

CONTENTS

INTRODUCTION

On February 13, 2006, my daughter died of an accidental drug overdose. Statistics tell us that more than seventy thousand young people under the age of twenty-four die every year in the United States. Whatever the cause of death, be it illness, a car accident, drowning, domestic violence, a casualty of foreign wars, suicide, or death by poisonous substances, the families of these young people are left devastated. Our culture does not support, nor does it understand, the tremendous grief of those left behind.

When this most heartrending of tragedies strikes, our comfort in the world and all that we thought we knew is shattered. And through this tear in the fabric of our everyday lives, we have the unique opportunity to catch a glimpse of another reality. We have the opportunity to stretch beyond our limited perceptions of life, into an expanded view of Life in the bigger sense.

In my own personal journey through grief, I have been blessed to receive the guidance and support of two extraordinary women, each of whom serve as a beacon of light in this world. They have dedicated their lives to uplifting humanity through their own unique gifts and in their own unique ways.

The Reverend Marian Starnes served as my counselor and spiritual advisor throughout my darkest days. Her unshakable spiritual foundation, based upon the knowledge that life never ends, only changes, and her complete trust in a loving and compassionate God gave me courage and comfort time and time again. I took the liberty of including excerpts from our taped conversations, knowing that her guidance and counsel will benefit many others.

I am grateful beyond what I can express for the opportunity to have studied for many years with Sue Gurnee at Growing Wheel International. If not for her dedication to understanding and teaching energetic principles in order to advance our self-awareness and to facilitate our own healing, I would have been ill prepared to work through my grief. It is a testament to Sue's invaluable work that I was able to survive and find fulfillment and joy in life again.

To both of these wonderful women, I will be forever grateful.

I must also acknowledge the unfailing support and encouragement of my son, Will Hess. He has stood witness to my journey, even as he traveled in his own way, and he cared for me in times of illness. We shared this experience, and in the sharing, the heavy burden became bearable. His devotion is an example of the triumph of love in our lives.

I do believe that the human spirit, by its very nature, has the innate ability to rise above restriction, limitation, despair, grief, incapacity, and in fact, the entire spectrum of circumstances that test our very will to survive.

I offer my personal story of grief and the possibility of transcendence for those who suffer the profound pain of loss with the hope that they may find comfort in the telling and courage to stretch beyond grief into the realization of a new life.

Anne Godar Hess

2010

Cover photograph: Kate Hess, age five

PROLOGUE

We are walking the Kabbalah trails, Will and I. On this day, our fifth in the Appalachian Mountains, I am struggling toward the highest point on this vibrational template of the Tree of Life. You see, I have been quite ill. I have been in constant pain for many months. My firstborn child is my companion in this journey. Will, at age twenty-eight, has the vitality and strength of youth. Today, my legs feel leaden, stiff, and strangely separate from the rest of my body. Each step is carefully considered. I have a walking stick on which I lean heavily as I inch upward on the steep and slippery incline.

It has been raining for several days, and under the pine needles and leaves is the dense red clay that threatens to propel me downhill with an unmeasured step. Will gives me his walking stick. Now I have two, to which I am clutching so tightly that my hands are becoming numb. We walk together, one slow, tentative step after another. I am breathing hard; the effort seems monumental.

"I don't think I can make it."

"Sure you can. Here, rest on this log, and I'll run ahead and see how much farther to the top."

He scampers up the hillside like a mountain goat, sure-footed and strong. I have no stamina. Breathing hard, I am reminded of the physical effort required for childbirth. Just as there is no turning back from the process of new life emerging, I know that I cannot turn back from this journey. I must continue on the path. Shortly, Will returns.

"Once you pass this group of fallen trees, the path isn't as steep. Here, come this way, it's not as slippery."

We move at a snail's pace. My body is exhausted, but I am determined to make it to the Crown. I banish all thoughts of getting down this same slope. Perhaps there is another way down. Will made it up on his own just the day before, but he did not travel down a different path.

Finally we reach the fallen trees. I must stop. I lean against a powerful tree that is angled just slightly down hill, just enough to cradle me within its strength and stability. I drink from my water bottle and breathe deeply.

A moment later, we hear someone coming up the path behind us.

Two lovely ladies from Switzerland yell up the hillside, "Anne, do you want your hat?"

"What?"

"You dropped your hat. We'll bring it up to you."

I am completely supported by this pillar of a tree. Shortly, Lisa and Edith arrive, only slightly out of breath. They tell us that they had started up a different path, much less well defined, but had to turn back before coming this way. They've been climbing for quite a while and they look energetic and vital. They are so strong, I think. Onward they go, and I must start up again too, Will following me in case I slip.

Edith yells down, "This is your Himalaya!" referring to the comment I had made the previous day as we were walking up the gentle incline leading to the frequency of the tenth sefirah. Then, I had said, "This is my Himalaya!" My brother, looking down at me from the small cabin at the center of this station on the Tree of Life, laughed and said, "I think the Crown is your Himalaya." Funny, funny.

We move along, the pain in my legs intense. I am completely supported by my two walking sticks. Suddenly, a thought pops into my head. Beethoven couldn't hear his masterpiece Ninth Symphony. He was profoundly deaf when he composed it. The sweet notes of the choral "Ode to Joy" come to mind like raindrops falling from heaven. I start humming: la, da da da de dum, de da da da de dum, de dum. I find that when I am humming the simple melody, the steps are easier. Step after step, I keep singing, imagining old Ludwig hearing the notes in his mind. I imagine him standing at the podium, while another conductor, one who is not deaf, actually leads the orchestra at the premiere of this great symphony. I imagine the old maestro, so enveloped in the rapture of his own inspired creation, that at the conclusion of the performance, he needs to be physically assisted to turn to the thunderous applause of the audience. Over and over, I hum and sing the "Ode to Joy." Soon, almost without realizing it, we have reached the top! Our two lovely Swiss ladies are quietly and respectfully standing, meditating on the rarified vibrations of the unmanifest endless potential, the Divine Intelligence. I lay down on the rocks, momentarily too exhausted to focus on the vibrations. All is quiet. This is sacred space.

෨෧

Joy! Fair Spark of the gods,
Daughter of Elysium!
Thy magic reunites those
Whom stern custom has parted.
"Ode to Joy"
F. Schiller

We start our descent from the highest point, still carefully placing each footstep, still humming Beethoven's great masterpiece. I am in great physical pain but my spirit soars. My thoughts turn to my little Kate at age four, running here and there, exclaiming "Oh joy!" her sweetness and innocence bubbling over, exuberant and playful. At the time, I thought, *what a strange thing for a child to say.* Now, I think, *how beautiful is the innocence of a child. How perfect is the Spirit that embodies our physical being.* I know without a doubt that I have turned a corner in my healing process. I have walked through the pain, the agony, and the devastation following the death of my daughter more than three years ago. Now I stand in the bright morning of a new day, a new life.

We reach our meeting place at the House of Five Senses and greet our fellow participants of this workshop offered by my friend, Sue Gurnee at Growing Wheel International, and introducing the frequencies of the eternal traditions of the Kabbalah. I share my account of our experience up the mountain and of my experience of profound joy as expressed through the genius of Ludwig van Beethoven. The great conductor, Joseph Krips, who recorded all of the Beethoven symphonies with the London Symphony Orchestra, once offered his personal vision of the finale of the Ninth. He believed that it simply does not take place here on earth, but in heaven. Surely, this must be true.

Soon, we are all listening to the fourth movement of the Ninth Symphony, including the choral of Schiller's "Ode to Joy". Waves of exquisitely beautiful sounds wash through, in, and around me, and I feel that I have reached a new level of awareness. I am overwhelmed with feelings of gratitude.

PART ONE

THE WANDERER

I.

Kate was almost always an enigma to me, my child, my Daughter of Elysium. I knew her so well, yet I hardly knew her at all. It was difficult to describe who she was because her character was so paradoxical. She was fragile, yet could be tough as nails. She was very fearful at times and utterly fearless at other times. She was extraordinarily willful and determined, but also considerate and protective of those she loved. She was sweet and gentle but could be explosive if triggered. She had ADHD and a diagnosed learning disability, specifically in language skills, yet she excelled at math. I never really understood how her mind worked. She was just wired differently. Still, she was charismatic, very charming, and she had an absolutely brilliant smile.

I almost lost her when she was little. Even now, recalling the memory, I shudder at the luck of it. There have been many times in my life when I have felt the presence of angels walking beside us, and this was surely one of those times. We were exploring the newly built shopping mall, Will, Kate, and I. Kate was only three years old, but there were so many things to see, so many exciting window displays full of color and varied textures, spotlights and piped music. I was growing impatient with Kate, as she would lag behind or wander ahead of us. She was independent, distractible. I was watchful. Will and I walked steadily together, Kate zigged and zagged. Will and I leisurely ambled to the shop across the way, and I watched to see that Kate would follow. We stopped and waited. Suddenly, she looked to where she expected us to be, but we weren't there. She screamed and bolted. In an instant, she was hurtling down the mall, passing shops like a sprinter in a mad dash to the finish line. She thought we had left her. My baby girl thought she was lost and alone. She ran for her life. She ran as fast as her legs could carry her, but she was running away from us. If I hadn't seen it, I would never have believed that a small child could disappear so fast.

Will and I took off after her in a race with a desperate three year-old. But she had a head start. People watched us fly past, a little girl screaming like a banshee, a woman and boy following, calling out the child's name.

"Kate! Kate! We're here! We haven't left you! Stop!"

Finally, an older woman walking toward us understood the situation immediately. I think she must have been an angel in human disguise, because she caught

Kate's attention and said, "There's your mommy, right behind you." Kate stopped and turned as we ran to her. In an instant, she was in my arms. Safe, not lost at all.

❧

Eighteen years passed after that day in the mall. Eighteen more birthday parties, Thanksgiving dinners, and Christmas celebrations. Eighteen more years of a shared life before Kate left this world. She slipped away quietly in the early morning hours of February 13, 2006, the drugs in her system slowing her breath until it stopped. My friend and spiritual advisor, Reverend Marian Starnes, told me that she crossed over with angels around her, that they lifted her straight out of this vibration. That she stayed long enough to fulfill her soul's contract and then she was called Home.

Can we really know our soul's intent? Was it my own Higher Self who, on that awful, quiet night that Kate left, whispered the words in my ear, "Kate is dead and you must now go on without her"? God is merciful. She left gently, her body untouched by trauma. Memories reside in a timeless place. I can recall all too well the devastation, the shock, the clenching pain of my loss.

"You haven't lost me, Mom. I'm still here."

Tell me again, Kate. Tell me a hundred times.

"I'm not lost. I'm here. Closer than I've ever been."

Closer than my own heartbeat. Not lost at all.

II.

I have always been what some would call highly sensitive. I feel energetic vibrations as bodily sensations, though I am not always aware of the origins of the sensations. I am primarily clairsentient, moderately clairaudient, and occasionally clairvoyant. For as long as I can remember, my approach to life has been deeply spiritual. For almost thirty years, I've used the technique of meditation to quiet the body, still the mind, and access the inner realms. In this way, I learned to pray, to focus my attention, and to listen to my inner guidance. This spiritual orientation has kept me from being completely overwhelmed by the vibrations of this world. I was raised in the Catholic faith, but I respect and embrace the spiritual truths found in all religions. Even with this unshakable spiritual foundation, Kate's death left me shattered. I had tried everything within my power to keep her alive and healthy, but in the end, I could not circumvent her soul's plan for its own ultimate healing.

Kate came into this world with very specific challenges. She was a difficult child to parent. Almost from the beginning, I noticed something about the way she would stare into space, eyes unfocused, that alerted me to something different about her. She was diagnosed with ADHD in 1992 when she was eight years old. At that time, there was limited understanding about this complex neurological disorder. There were even child development and medical experts who questioned the validity of such a disorder, insisting that it was all a myth and that poor parenting was to blame for much of the out-of-control behavior, impulsivity, lack of attention, and poor social skills that some children were exhibiting.

I didn't give these experts much credence. Clearly, they didn't have a child who could do a hundred handstands against the wall and then twirl about the room until everyone around her was dizzy. Clearly, they couldn't have had personal experience with a child who had problems sleeping for days on end, year after year, or who would stare into space in a world of her own so much of the time. And especially, most especially, they couldn't have had personal, daily experience with a child who was so impulsive that I feared for her safety, always wondering what she might do next with never a thought of consequences. In the mid 1990's, researchers were just beginning to piece together the complex neurological physiology behind ADHD.

As much as I focused on Kate's behavior, ever alert for subtle clues as to what was going on in her mind, I loved being a mother. I cherished those early years when I was fortunate to stay home with both Will and Kate. I have precious memories of rocking babies to sleep and reading Dr. Seuss and Winnie the Pooh books every day. There were swimming lessons in the summertime and karate lessons for several years. There were school activities and homemade Halloween costumes. I have so many precious memories. But after my divorce when Will and Kate were in elementary school, I had to go back to work as a dental hygienist. I became a single mother when Kate was seven years old. I lived the life of many single parents, juggling the day-to-day needs of the children with the immediate necessity of providing financial stability for us. Will and Kate's dad remained a presence in their lives, and Kate lived with her dad for about a year when she was in high school. My parents lived nearby, and both Will and Kate were fortunate to grow up knowing their grandparents well. Our lives were not unlike many families today. We were not the traditional nuclear family; there were serious tensions here and there. Still, we were very close and supportive.

Every year in July, we spent a week at the beach for a large family reunion. Grandparents, aunts and uncles, cousins, extended family and friends all came. We looked forward all year to these special vacations. Kate rode the waves and got brown as a nut in the sun. We'd all take turns preparing dinners. Will and Kate both took their turns, sometimes making a salad, sometimes a special dessert. Whenever I made an especially good dish, Kate would boast that she had made it, getting up at dawn to gather and prepare the ingredients. She was quick with a joke. Those were good times.

There were ups and downs during the school years. Kate did well when she had a good teacher, someone who genuinely enjoyed teaching and helping young students succeed. But even the best teachers couldn't help her master her weak reading and writing skills. Despite vision therapy to help her eyes work in sync while reading and special classes to develop organizational skills, she struggled with the English language. Still, she persevered and had ambitions for college. She set her sights on a major in statistics, having enjoyed and done well in all of her high school math courses.

Sometimes Kate's impulsivity worked in her favor. When she was sixteen, she applied for an Outward Bound scholarship sponsored by a service program at the high school. I found out about it after she won the scholarship, and I was thrilled to buy her hiking boots, a backpack, and other supplies. She spent ten days in western North Carolina rock climbing, rappelling down steep cliff walls, and hiking. She also enjoyed going to summer camp sponsored by ARE (The Association for Research and Enlightenment) where she slept in a rustic cabin without electricity and ate vegetarian food. I was always surprised by her strong constitution. Sometimes I'd wake up in the morning to find that she had rearranged the furniture in her room. I'd always wonder how she could possibly be strong enough to move the heavy bed and bookcase by herself.

Both Will and Kate had jobs in their teen years. Will worked consistently in various restaurants as a waiter. Kate held a variety of jobs. Her first was in a pet store when she was fifteen years old. She worked at a takeout pizza place and as an associate in a women's clothing store. She was a "hood tech" at Jiffy Lube; she sold bagels at Bruegger's. She worked in the office of a heating and air-conditioning company; she did computer data entry at a local nightclub. She became a licensed insurance agent while attending classes full-time at the local community college. And she almost always had a boyfriend. She was happiest when she was in love. Our lives were full and busy as she'd float here and there, in and out of the house. Always somewhere to go, always some new thing to do. Mostly happy, or so I thought. Mostly happy, until her life became more and more complicated.

ᏆᏇ

I tell you these things so that you may have an understanding of who Kate was. When a young person dies, everyone wants to know what happened. I can't tell you of her later troubles without an explanation of who she was. I want to tell you how funny she was and how sweet she could be. I want to tell you how she had a stubborn streak, for good or ill, and how she could so cleverly taunt Will in the unique love-hate style of siblings. I want to tell you how frustrated she was at times and how frustrating she was to us when we couldn't reason with her. I want to tell you how beautiful she was and how very much she was loved.

Many people with attention deficit hyperactivity disorder have an increased risk of substance abuse in a misguided attempt to balance their unbalanced brain chemistry. Of the six identified ADHD types, those who fit into the classic category, like Kate, with impaired prefrontal cortex activity in the brain and resulting poor impulse control, are especially at risk. I believe this is why she started using drugs. It was a way to self-medicate, to bring relief during difficult times when she couldn't cope with her problems. But this short-lived relief always leads to more complications and even more disordered brain chemistry, as well as the very real risk of addictions.

Kate sought help from many health-care professionals during the last eighteen months of her life. She saw psychiatrists, psychologists, social workers, and addiction specialists. There were multiple trips to the emergency room for overdoses, hospital admissions for treatment and observation, and two extended stays in rehab facilities. She was prescribed antiseizure medications, antipsychotic medications, various antidepressant medications, and numerous antianxiety medications in large quantities. At various times, these specialists diagnosed Kate with post-traumatic stress disorder, bipolar disorder, panic disorder, psychosis, depression, poly-substance abuse, and borderline personality disorder. None of these specialists identified and addressed her real problems. But they did write mega-prescriptions with minimal oversight. Over time, Kate became more and more unstable. She was being progressively poisoned by pharmaceutical drugs. She was being primed for destruction. And I felt so afraid, so helpless to save her.

III.

What parent can contemplate the death of her child for more than a fraction of a second? It took only a fraction of a second for me to dismiss the small voice in my head late on the night of February 12 that said, "Kate is dead and you must now go on without her." I banished that voice to a place of temporary amnesia. It wasn't until many weeks later that I pulled the message from its slumber of hibernation and began to question its source. But by then, there were no answers, for I was in a state of profound shock.

February 13, 2006, began like many other Monday mornings. It was the start of a new work week. I awoke, showered, dressed, and ate a small breakfast. It has always been my habit to take a few minutes every morning to ground myself and balance my energies for the day ahead. This day during my short meditation, I noticed something different. In my mind's eye, I saw a lovely, soft, very white light in front of me. I had never seen this before. I could not integrate this energy with my own. I realized that it was self-contained. So I just enjoyed its presence for a few moments. And then I went about my day.

It was at 10:30 that morning, just after I had seen my third patient of the day, when my boss pulled me into our small consultation room. A very large man wearing a black leather jacket sat in the corner. He identified himself as a detective with the police department. My mind was already going into shock as I sat facing him, my boss standing by my side. After verifying my identity, this detective very quietly told me that my daughter had "expired" early that morning at a local hospital. There was a suspicion of drug involvement. Her body was being transferred to the medical examiner's office for autopsy.

I could barely comprehend this. I had seen Kate through so many close calls, and now she was gone and I had not been by her side? How could this be? I don't know how I continued to function that day. Our office manager drove me home and stayed with me until Will arrived. I fought panic as I realized the terrible phone calls that I needed to make.

My first thought was to call Sue Gurnee. I had studied with Sue and worked very closely with her for more than a decade, and she had helped Kate many times in the previous years. I knew that with her high sense perceptions, she could help Kate now. I was too unstable to even begin to contemplate where Kate was or what condition she was in, but I knew that Sue could step in and do whatever was necessary to assure that Kate was given the support and guidance that she needed in the spiritual world. Knowing that Kate would be taken care of, I turned my attention to other calls. I was on autopilot, shock protecting me from the full realization of what had happened. I dreaded having to make the call to Kate's dad, my ex-husband,

Curt, and somehow find the words to tell him that our daughter was gone. My heart broke as I made the call. Though we had had our differences over the years, all conflict dissolved like a puff of smoke in the wind. I knew how much he loved his children. His pain was as great as mine.

I called my parents and my brother; I spoke to my brother-in-law who called my sister in Hawaii where she was attending a medical conference. I called Kate's boyfriend; I told my neighbors. Friends came by. I don't know how I was able to go on. I couldn't think of eating, but I drank water continuously. In the evening, Curt arrived from Annapolis, and that awful day ended with the three of us, Will, Curt, and me, sitting in my living room, trying to piece together what had happened and wondering "What do we do now?"

I slept fitfully that night, waking over and over again with tears streaming down my face. I never realized that we can cry in our sleep. The next morning, Will and I met with Curt and we began to face the multiple tasks ahead of us. The three of us spoke with a funeral director who advised us of the services he could offer, services of which we had no previous experience. I wrote a simple obituary and found the perfect dress for Kate to be clothed in for viewing. We discussed the specifics of the memorial service with the minister, and Will and Curt prepared their eulogies. We enlarged and framed our favorite photographs to be placed around the reception area. I functioned on pure adrenaline. Family began to gather from various parts of the country. Kate's friends began to call me hoping that the rumors they had heard were not true.

I remember every detail of Kate's memorial service. For months I replayed every scene in my mind. I would see Kate's body prepared so beautifully in the white formal gown she had worn to a school dance. I could hear my son, looking so handsome in his new suit, reminding us all that energy cannot be destroyed, it only changes form, and that Kate's beauty and brilliance survives. I could hear Curt's beautiful tribute to his daughter, telling us all who she was with such poignant simplicity. Over and over, these images played in my mind, for the reality of this event was too great for me to comprehend.

IV.

The weeks following Kate's memorial service are clouded in my memory. I functioned minimally. For many months, I hardly slept. My body was in a netherworld of stress and shock. My doctor prescribed sleeping pills and a mild tranquilizer for anxiety.

Within a week and a half, I had returned to work, though I was ill prepared to interact in any personal way with my patients. My coworkers were sensitive and accommodating, but the truth is, nobody knew what to say to me, so we all just went about our duties the best we could. I came home every night and couldn't stop the flood of tears.

Several weeks prior to Kate's death, Will had moved home temporarily in order to save enough money to move into a new apartment. I now asked him to stay with me for a while. I needed his presence. I needed him near me, and I wanted to be there for him during his time of confusion and grief. We were both adrift in the hurricane-force winds of shock, trauma, and disbelief. My family, my parents, my brother and sister, called almost daily to check in with us. Several of Kate's friends continued to call, nobody understanding how and why this had happened. What would have been Kate's twenty-second birthday came just three weeks after she died. I don't remember much of anything about that day. I was too lost in my fog of grief.

Soon, an envelope from the medical examiner's office arrived in the mail. "These are the remains of a slender, well-developed and –nourished appearing white female..." I was horrified to read the autopsy report. I felt that these people had desecrated my child's beautiful body without my permission, and at the exact time that I was being notified of her death. My sensitivities could only allow me to see this as the ultimate violation of the human body. I thought, how can people do such work? How can they dehumanize and depersonalize her, she who had been so alive just hours before? How can they dissect, weigh, and catalogue her internal organs? It was an assault to all of my senses, and I sank deeper into a pain so profound that it could ultimately only be described as torture. I was in a place of no-time and no-space. I needed to step away from this harsh, new reality in order to survive. I could only peek at it in small doses before I had to retreat again into the façade of everyday life.

V.

It was about six weeks after Kate's death as I was lying down to bed one night, when I decided to try to reach out to her. I was wondering where she was and what she was experiencing in the spiritual world. I thought, if we can send messages everyday to people on the other side of the world via e-mail, why couldn't I send a "special delivery" message to Kate?

All of a sudden and to my great surprise, her voice was inside my head! "Hi, Mom!" I could hardly believe it! Her voice was as clear as if we were talking on the telephone. She assured me that she was all right and in a beautiful place where she was being helped to regain her strength after losing so much of her vital force while in the body. This place was earthlike in its pristine beauty, with tall, mature trees and meadows with many varieties of flowers overlooking a deep, clear lake. There were many souls with her being attended to with loving care by special healers chosen for such work. Everyone had their own little private, cottage-like space in which to rest after various treatments and exercises.

I checked in with Kate nightly, and my communications with her were a healing balm for my broken heart.

VI.

Memories reside in a timeless place: *How can you really be gone? I can still hear your voice in my head, clear as day. I still think you'll be walking in the front door any minute now, phone pressed to your ear, talking to your friends.*

"Hi, Mom. How are you doing?"

Oh, you know, not so good.

"It'll get better. I promise."

Kate, do you remember when you were little, maybe five years old? You'd look for all sorts of cozy hiding places. You'd arrange the pillows and blankets on your bed into a fort. Or you'd burrow into the wardrobe or closet. I'd find you and you'd have a sheepish grin on your face, as if to say, "I've discovered a fun game." Espionage! Reconnaissance missions! Tricks up your sleeve! Remember when Grandma and Grandpa came to visit and Grandma thought she might help you clean up your room? How many of Will's toys did she find tucked away under your bed? Outrage! Grandma blew your cover. I hear you laughing. What a fun game!

Or how about that time you had no money to buy me a birthday gift? You found some old coins in a metal Band-aid can, long forgotten and tucked away in the back of a dresser drawer. You thought I'd like to have them all polished up, shiny as new. Pennies, dimes, nickels, and quarters, all shining like jewels. Then you put them back in that old beat-up

Band-aid can and wrapped it all up in paper with Happy Birthday balloons on it. Funny, funny! You were hilarious. You gave me the gift of laughter.

But they're not all good memories, are they Kate?

"No, Mom, they're not. But it'll get better. I promise."

∽

In truth, the trauma to my system from some memories is palpable. There were many times in Kate's life when she felt overwhelmingly discouraged and depressed, times when she longed for relief from the pain of dark emotions that she couldn't resolve. But only once did she attempt to escape from her pain with an act that could have easily resulted in her ultimate self-destruction.

She was three weeks out of her first twenty-eight day rehab program for multiple drug addictions, and we were celebrating my birthday with dinner at a festival sponsored every year by a local church. Kate had been subdued all day, and I watched her closely as I sat across the table from her. When she raised her arm to tuck her hair behind her ear, I noticed several thin cuts that she had made across her wrist, barely visible under her long-sleeved sweater. At that moment, my heart sank. Little inconsistencies that I had taken notice of the previous night started to fit together. I remembered that the Tylenol was missing when I went looking for it in the middle of the night. I remembered that Kate said, "I love you, Mom" when she saw that I was awake so late. I said, "I love you, too," but I thought it was an odd thing to say just out of the blue like that at three o'clock in the morning.

Now, almost twelve hours later, the realization of what had happened struck me hard in the pit of my stomach. Sitting across from her, in barely a whisper, I asked, "Did you take Tylenol?" She slowly nodded yes. I mouthed the words, "How much?" She silently formed the words, "A lot." I sat there in shock, hardly daring to believe that this was real. Kate knew what too much Tylenol could do to her liver. We quietly got up to leave, making apologies to my parents, saying that Kate wasn't feeling well, and Will and I took her immediately to the emergency room.

Kate was in the hospital for four days, where it was determined that she had taken twenty-five thousand milligrams of Tylenol. Without timely medical intervention, I believe her liver would have failed. And without help from my friend, Anna, a very gifted intuitive and energy worker, and Sue Gurnee, whom I was able to contact in Germany, I believe that Kate's liver could not have fully recovered. I later found out that within several days of her release from rehab, she had relapsed, and that this was a precipitating factor in her decision to deliberately overdose and end her life.

At the time, I didn't know that most addicts relapse over and over again before they are finally able to free themselves from the grip of their addictions. I didn't fully understand the vicious circle of addiction when Kate was alive. I was naïve in my belief that the way to conquer addictions required simply employing the will to stop. Now I understand that addictive substances actually change the chemistry of the brain. Additionally, in sentient moments, an addict experiences such remorse, self-hate, and regret, that she is driven to continue numbing these painful feelings. Returning home after that first night of Kate's hospitalization, I found notes that she had written and left on the desk in her room. In her note to me, she said that she loved me and that I had done everything I could do to help her, but she felt hopeless and the pain was too great for her to crawl out of the pit that she was in. Only a parent whose child has experienced such desperation can understand the gut-wrenching fear I felt.

So began several months of psychiatric evaluations. Kate was in and out of several hospitals and mental health facilities, and she voluntarily submitted to another fourteen-day rehab program. During this time, multiple psychotropic medications were prescribed, most of which only further complicated her recovery. It was six months before Kate was able to get off of this roller coaster and start rebuilding her life. Depression still lingered, but she was determined to cope by taking only one antidepressant medication that proved to provide some measure of relief.

Yes, these are hard memories to recall, and harder still to write about. But the truth requires all of our courage and bravery.

For a while, Kate seemed to be doing better. The antidepressant that she continued to take appeared to be helping. She was starting to look to her future with some hope, until she had a frightening car accident late one night driving home from a concert. Though she was unhurt, her car was totaled. Soon, she started experiencing flashbacks and panic attacks. She complained of back pain. Her medication was becoming less effective. The stress associated with dealing with the legal consequences of the accident was taking its toll.

By January of 2006, she decided that she again needed help from the psychiatrist who had treated her the previous year. He was unavailable, but on referral from the hospital where she was admitted after a particularly intense panic attack, an appointment was made with this psychiatrist's assistant, who was a psychotherapist and physician's assistant.

Unfortunately, this psychotherapist did not read the referral information from the hospital, nor were Kate's previous records available in the office for him to review. He gave her some samples of a second antidepressant, wrote a prescription for something to help her sleep and a second prescription for ninety Klonopin, a benzodiazepine for anxiety. I was shocked that Kate had received so many Klonopin, because this was the type of drug that she had previously overdosed on, resulting in a four day black-out and subsequent hospitalization. This was the type of drug for which she had entered rehab the previous year. I knew what these drugs could do to her. I knew that after taking three or four or more of these pills, she lost rational thought and could quickly spiral out of control, her impulsivity uncontained. I was beside myself with worry. I considered contacting the psychotherapist, but Kate assured me that she could handle it this time. She promised me that she was only taking it as prescribed.

Two weeks after receiving these medications, Kate fatally overdosed, the multiple drugs in her system slowing her breathing until it stopped.

PART TWO

JOURNEY TO THE FAR LANDS

I.

I first met Reverend Marian Starnes in 1993, not long after my divorce. I was still adjusting to my new life as a single mother, so on the advice of a friend, I requested a personal counseling session. Marian is the primary minister of a non-denominational church called The Brigade of Light, located in a beautiful two hundred acre retreat center in the Blue Ridge Mountains of North Carolina. Throughout the 1990's, Marian traveled regularly to Raleigh to speak of spiritual matters to a small gathering of people, and I arranged to meet her during one of these visits.

I was immediately comfortable in her presence. Not only is Marian an ordained minister with an unshakable spiritual foundation, she is also gifted with psychic perceptions. She is able to counsel people in a personal manner by tuning into their soul's energy. I met with her several times in the following years, and Will, Kate, and I also visited her at Terra Nova Center, her retreat center in the mountains. Over the years, I learned that Marian had suffered many personal losses, including the death of her adult son, a troubled Vietnam veteran, in the 1980's.

Though I had not seen Marian for several years, I now felt compelled to call her. I needed her counsel and comfort. We made arrangements to get together on her next visit to Raleigh, just eight weeks after Kate's death. She appeared much as I remembered her, alert and vital, though she was now in her late seventies. She hugged me and I felt the compassion of a mother who knew, who had experienced, the pain I felt.

We began our session with a short prayer, asking for absolute Truth and only Truth, to be given voice. Marian then told me, "Kate is safely back in the Father's house. She is in Paradise. She came in with a super-sensitive system that simply could not handle poisonous substances of any kind. She was a star child and the vibration of this earth was just more than she could handle. There is no stigma attached to this; all there is, is great rejoicing that she is Home. She is in Paradise.

"But I need to tell you this, she only came for twenty-one years, she only came for a brief time. There is absolutely nothing you could have done to prevent this, nothing her family or friends could have done. When I had my initial contact with her, she said that it was very, very important for you to know that this was not the way she had planned it. Actually, her demise was to come through a car wreck, but noth-ing here is as it seems. We don't always get to call the shots. She had no intent to inflict this much pain on the people she loved. But she was really clear that there was no more time.

"She is not in any way earthbound, but she is very psychically connected with you. There are absolutely no words that I can speak to you that will heal the hurt. Only time can do that. Right now, time is your dearest companion. Spirit is Spirit. It never ends, it only changes."

II.

Throughout that spring and into the summer, the days passed slowly. I had moved all of Kate's belongings, all the many boxes of clothing that Will and I had collected from her apartment, up to her old room and closed the door. I simply couldn't face sorting through it all, touching her clothes, some of which still held her scent. I also placed the urn containing her ashes in her room. I didn't know what to do with it; it was too painful to contemplate. It was Will's presence that got me up every day. I thank God that he was with me. I forced myself to function, if only minimally.

I went to work. I paid my bills. I didn't cook, I didn't clean house. I neglected the yard work. Nobody told me how much grief can physically hurt. My body was exhausted from the continuous stress I was under, and I couldn't relax. Every day I read the obituaries, surprised at how many young people die that I had never taken notice of before. I worried about Will, fearful for his safety. I didn't care what I ate; I think we lived on fast food and takeout. I had to pretend that I was all right in order to function, but family birthdays, Mother's Day, and our annual beach trip were all tortuous. My family didn't know how to help me, but I relied on their constant presence.

What kept me going were my nightly visits with Kate. To hear her voice in my head, if only for a few minutes before I fell into a fitful sleep, helped me survive this awful time.

One night as I lay down, closed my eyes, and journeyed to what I now called the Healing Place, I found Kate in her little cottage, lying quietly on her bed. I sensed that she felt discouraged and regretful for certain events in her life. I went to her and lay down beside her. Without a word, she turned to me and put her head on my shoulder.

I wrapped my arms around her to comfort her, and said, "Life can be very hard. Sometimes it can seem as insurmountable as climbing the highest place on earth, Mount Everest in the Himalayas. I read about the early explorers and the challenges they faced. I read about how they first had to trek many miles on foot to reach the base of the mountain. Then they would spend weeks at a base camp to get acclimated to the lack of oxygen at that high altitude. Their first trip up the mountain was through the icefall, which is a treacherous area of ice towers and wide, deep fissures. These brave explorers crossed these deep cracks in the ice over ladders bolted together. Some of these fissures are so deep that they couldn't even see the bottom, and to fall would surely have been fatal."

I felt the presence of many souls watching us, listening to every word I said. Kate kept her head on my shoulder, and I knew that she was listening intently. "The weather can be unforgiving. The winds can reach hurricane force with little warning. But these brave explorers pushed on. They climbed without the aid of fixed ropes and used sharp picks to inch up vertical walls of slick ice. Unexpected storms sometimes forced them to turn back. There was no shame in turning back, for if the conditions were not in their favor, it would have been foolhardy to continue. These brave men faced unimaginable challenges, but eventually, despite all the danger and despite all the hardship, the very highest place on this earth, the summit of Mount Everest was won!"

Kate looked up at me and gave me a beautiful smile. I continued, "Life can sometimes be this hard. Our own personal challenges can seem just as daunting, just as treacherous, as if we were actually climbing the tallest mountain. And we can only do the best we are capable of. You did the very best you could during your life on earth. You loved much and gave great joy and happiness to those around you, and now it's time to rest."

I held her tightly and she was happy.

III.

In our culture, it is generally thought that the grieving process takes about a year, and then we just get on with our lives. I found this to be an outrageously false presumption. For the entire first year after Kate's death, I remained in a paradoxical state of unrelenting trauma and shocked disbelief. I felt shattered into a million pieces, without the first clue of how to put the pieces back together. Somehow I managed to continue to go to work by putting my fragile self on pause, pretending to be normal, only to press the play button again at the end of each workday. Curt and I worked together to administer Kate's estate. I sold her car to pay off her debts, and we made several trips to the courthouse to close the estate.

I dreaded the coming of my birthday in September and would have skipped it altogether if my family had not insisted on a very small dinner celebration. By November, my parents had convinced me that we needed to find a final resting place for Kate's urn, and I gratefully accepted their gift of a small burial plot in the closest cemetery. We had our Thanksgiving dinner in a restaurant that year, for I couldn't face our usual home-cooked celebration. With some time off from work at the Christmas holidays, I decided that I finally needed to sort through the many boxes of clothes stacked in Kate's old room. But I knew that I couldn't do it alone. I called my sister, Jeanne, in Wisconsin and asked her to come to Raleigh to help me.

When we were small children, before my brother was born, I would stand at the screen door every day waiting for Jeanne to come home from school. I'd stand there patiently every afternoon and when I'd see her walking down the street, I'd run to tell my mom, "Jeannie's coming!" I'd then run back to the screen door and wait anxiously until she walked into the house. I was so happy to see her, even though she had been gone for only a few hours. This was my memory as I waited for Jeanne to come home for the holidays that year. I needed my sister now. So Jeanne, who was with us at Kate's birth, spent her Christmas helping me tackle the task of sorting through and clearing out Kate's room. I kept only a few items of special significance.

Even in the midst of their own grief, my family stood by to support me. And even knowing how much I was loved and cared for, the raw pain of that first year took its toll. The unrelenting stress combined with the lack of sleep, caused a breakdown of sorts. I was physically exhausted, my immune system so compromised, that the chicken pox virus from my childhood was reactivated and I came down with shingles. I was forced to rest, still bearing the shock of my loss.

IV.

As the first anniversary of Kate's death approached, I made the decision to visit Marian at Terra Nova Center in the mountains. It had been years since I had been there, but even in the grayness of the February winter, it was still a beautiful and peaceful place. I had found a lovely angel garden statue that I wanted to set somewhere on the grounds in Kate's memory, and Will and I walked through the gardens to find the perfect spot. During that visit, we both had the opportunity to sit with Marian again and hear her counsel.

After a short prayer to align with Truth, Marian told me, "Do not be in such a hurry to go through all the grieving process because it cannot and will not be denied. There are things your body will go through; it's part of the process. It takes at least two years for the molecular structure of the body to recover from a hit such as you've had. The cells of your body have got to heal, because this hit wasn't just your heart, it wasn't just your spirit, it wasn't just your emotions, it was your body too. It's like having broken ribs. You can't rush it; the healing takes its own time. Your spiritual knowledge has been your saving grace. That's what's been getting you through this. But no matter how much you knew, your nervous and emotional systems still erupted."

I knew from my regular contact with Kate that she had graduated from the Healing Place and now was in a place of light and joy. I could not follow her activities with the same level of contact that I had enjoyed previously, but I knew that she had regained her vital essence and could now be of service to others.

Marian continued, "Kate remembers nothing of the pain; she only remembers the love. You gave her exactly what she needed so that she could complete her contract. And now she has work to do. She's just been given the assignment to work with people who have died suddenly as children in acts of violence: a drive-by shooting, a drug overdose, a car wreck. She's in the Welcoming Center, which means that she can't be with you every single minute. Not as the Spirit that she is. But the essence of her that embodied as Kate is with you to comfort you and strengthen you. She's as close as your own heartbeat. You have been given an opportunity to take a giant step into the realization of our own immortality. That is what we are here to learn. I AM immortal. We are immortal Spirit."

V.

Will and I returned home and for a while life continued much as before. I was relieved that the first year of grief was behind me, but remembering Marian's words describing a two year recovery, the prospect of another year of unrelenting pain seemed overwhelming.

I went to work every day but I felt fundamentally different from my coworkers and patients. I was fortunate to work in a personable office, but now all the social pleasantries worked against me. I felt raw in my grief. I felt separate from everyone who enjoyed healthy families and good fortune. I felt like I had failed in the one area of my life that was most dear to my heart, that of being a good parent. I couldn't keep my daughter alive, much less healthy, happy, and fulfilled. And I felt tremendous anger toward those who had prescribed so many psychotropic medications without considering the effects these drugs had on Kate in her most vulnerable state.

During this time, my allergies worsened dramatically and I developed sciatica. The pain in my lower back and down my leg was intense, and the tension in my muscles at the end of the workday prevented any hope of restorative sleep. I noticed that my hair was thinning, a symptom of chronic, unrelenting stress. I had never been one to drink much alcohol beyond the rare glass of wine with dinner, but now I had a glass of scotch almost every evening. Will seemed to be doing better than I, but I still worried about him. He never discussed his feelings, and I could only hope that he was recovering from his loss.

I continued to find things around the house that had belonged to Kate: jewelry, cards and letters that she had kept, hair clips, even envelopes of her hair that she had tucked away after haircuts. One envelope contained a twelve inch ponytail. In her mid-teens, she had dyed her naturally dark brown hair to black, but after she tired of it and realized that the color couldn't be removed by any chemical means, she submitted to cutting it out in one fell swoop. Another envelope held a shorter ponytail from when she had impulsively cut her own hair when she was ten years old. I loved Kate's hair. It was thick and full and soft to the touch. I took her to a salon on the day of her first prom. The stylist studied her long, smooth, dark hair and then went to work. Elaborate braided strands swirled into an up-do, and sparkly hairpins held it all in place. Kate loved it, and I told her that she looked like a Grecian goddess. I think she felt like a queen all night.

So many memories came flooding back and I felt lost in my pain.

VI.

Weeks went by. I was drifting. Visions appeared in my dreams.

I am in a little submarine bubble that lands very gently on the sandy ocean floor, just like the lunar module softly landing on the surface of the moon. Softly enough so it does not disturb the velvety, fine lunar dust. I am reminded of astronaut Buzz Aldrin's description of the lunar landscape as "magnificent desolation". At first glance, the bottom of the ocean looks this way - quiet, dark, and empty. But I know it is not.

As my eyes adjust to the darkness and I look more closely, I see that it has its own ecosystem, much different from what I know of light and air and earth. Strange creatures reside here, with odd shapes unlike anything I have seen before. Some dart about in jerky bursts of energy; some are graceful in a slow-motion ballet. In their effort to avoid predators, some creatures camouflage themselves. Some hide in, around, and under objects that litter the ocean floor. Some sleep with their eyes open, ever alert to danger. There are even luminous creatures in this place, their colors glowing in the dark. Even at this depth, light exists. It is mesmerizing. All around me there is life where I thought there was only empty space. And I absorb it all, until it is time to return to the surface and awaken from this dream.

Not all of my dreams were as benign as this one. I began to have nightmares, too. In these dreams, I was washed away in floodwaters, rolling and tumbling along with a force that I had no control over. I had recurring dreams of a lion or tiger loose in the house. In terror, I'd frantically try to find a room that I could hide in, someplace where I'd be protected from the danger lurking quietly just around the corner.

I realized that I didn't feel safe in this world anymore. I felt vulnerable. This world, this life, seemed threatening, hostile, and foreboding. And in my fear, I separated myself even more from all meaningful social contact.

VII.

"Don't run away!" my dear friend, Marian Starnes, admonished me. "Right now you'd like to bolt and run. But if you're the person I think you are, you will not bolt and run. You will stand your ground, take your hits, and know the truth about what's really happening."

Marian was right. I did want to run away. I wanted to go to some isolated cabin in the woods where I wouldn't have to speak to anyone. I wanted to rent a cottage on the coast of Nova Scotia and just be alone. I wanted to get in my car and drive until I could find a quiet, dark spot to hide in.

"You are going through a process that is hitting every nerve you've got. No stone will be left unturned. No issue will be left unresolved. No hurt will be left unhealed. Know the truth! Allow the energy to take you along instead of pushing it, knowing absolutely and totally that we are immortal Spirit. You have got to take the spiritual substance and mix it with your soul's understanding, your emotions, your mind, and your physical body. There is no shortcut."

No, I thought, *I can't run away*.

I was determined to focus my attention on getting through each day, one at a time. I still occasionally made contact with Kate and found that we could communicate thoughts without resorting to placing them within the context of words. We simply shared an understanding of a concept.

I realized that the totality of our Spirit exists on a much grander scale than we can imagine. Life is so much more than our present orientation in time and space leads us to believe. Kate and I have shared many lifetimes on this earth plane, our souls having incarnated together in various relationships. But in this lifetime, in this here and now, she is my Kate and I am her mom. And so we continued to address each other in this way.

I found that as time passed, there were some days when I actually felt all right. The grief would lesson a bit, and every once in a while, I'd even find myself laughing at a joke I'd heard that struck me as funny. Other days I fell back into the depression so characteristic of grief. But even on my darkest days, there was a part of me that stood off to the side, reminding me that this was all a process and that I would get through it just fine.

Our family gathering at the beach this second year was easier, but there were still moments when I would retreat, incapable of relaxing in the midst of a large number of people. I was grateful that my family was so understanding. I was still tentative. I was far from being healed of this terrible heartache, but I was making progress.

VIII.

It had been almost a year and a half since Kate left us, and again I felt the need to visit Marian at her retreat center in the mountains. I visited Kate's angel statue. It was as I left it, lovely and serene in one of the peaceful gardens on the property. I was glad to see Marian. I was grateful for her guidance and comfort, for I knew that she was well-acquainted with grief. She had survived so much of her own personal loss. What she told me, however, took me by surprise.

Again, after a short prayer to align with the spirit of Truth, she said, "You have done a good job of walking through the sorrow and the grief, but it is now time for celebration. It is also time to let the Kate that you knew move on, for there is great work that she can do, and to simply remember the beauty of the spirit that moved and lived and was with you for that period of time. You don't need Kate as a crutch. You can stand now above and beyond the sorrow. As you move into this new year, you will find the strength that you never dreamed that you had. You will not have to look to this or to that; you will find it within yourself, for you are about to make a great discovery. That which you know as Will, that which you knew as Kate, are nothing more than the God part of you yourself, for you are all one in Spirit.

"I am getting the most beautiful image of a Rainbow Bridge going off into the mists. It is beckoning you to 'Come walk the Rainbow Path, for there are miracles and wonders you haven't even dreamed of.' It is time not to look over your shoulder to where you have been, but to know that as you cross this Rainbow Bridge, it is going to take you Home - back into the vast ISness.

"The one who was your daughter is getting closer and closer to the vast ISness. She says, 'I must go up the mountain. I must go to another level and you must let me go.' Through her work, it is as if she is at the bottom of the crystal mountain. She is doing wonderful work, yet one day she too will go up this mountain. When you cross over, it will be as if you were never apart from her. There has been absolutely no judgment of any kind for the decisions she made. All there is, is great rejoicing that she is Home. The spirit that was Kate, you wouldn't recognize her now, not with these eyes. But with your soul, you will know her instantly. She is wearing rainbow colors, and you now stand at the crossroads."

I didn't understand this at all. What is the Rainbow Bridge? What is the crossroads?

"The crossroads is a place of change. You can do this. You are a real woman."

IX.

I returned home in a daze. I was confused and I prayed for understanding. One day it suddenly dawned on me that the Rainbow Bridge is a metaphor for the chakra system! The seven chakras of the ancient Indian yogic tradition represent the organization of life force energy as it manifests from Spirit into the physical plane.[1] The word *chakra* literally translates as 'spinning wheel of energy'. The chakra system represents various states of consciousness, from the physical awareness of the first chakra located at the base of the spine, to the enlightenment of Divine consciousness entering through the seventh chakra at the top of the head. These various levels of vibration manifest through the color spectrum. The Rainbow Bridge is a metaphor for the evolution of consciousness!

In Genesis, it is written, "And God said, this is the token of the covenant which I make between Me and you and every living creature that is with you, for perpetual generations: I do set My bow in the cloud, and it shall be for a token of a covenant between Me and the earth. And it shall come to pass, when I bring a cloud over the earth, that the bow shall be seen in the cloud: And I will remember my covenant, which is between Me and you and every living creature of all flesh."[2]

A compassionate God has given us a map for transformation!

I also began to understand that the crystal mountain that Marian had referred to symbolized the higher states of consciousness. From my interest in the early explorers' attempts to reach the summit of Mount Everest, I had learned that Buddhist philosophy regards the mountain as the zenith of consciousness. The mountain is "the physical expression of a higher state of being that exists beyond and outside time and space, a kind of pure understanding." [3]

Everything was becoming much clearer to me.

X.

My focus was no longer on Kate, for I knew that she was experiencing the freedom and joy of the spiritual realms, unimaginable to us still embodied here on earth. Rather, I turned my attention to my own healing.

I had worked at length with the energetics of the chakra system, having studied with Sue Gurnee since the mid 1990's. Sue is an extraordinary woman, the daughter of professional cave explorers. As a child, she accompanied her parents deep into the darkest, subterranean worlds where she honed her innate sensitivities and high sense perceptions. She grew up with world-class scientists, explorers, and adventurers around the dinner table. Eventually, after years of dedicated study, she developed a systematic way to work in the vibrational realm of cause, in order to manifest change in the physical world. Over the years, I had attended more than twenty-five workshops offered by Sue and I had done much work to correct patterns of imbalance. We always approached this work "gracefully and easily" by learning dowsing techniques and trusting in the process that Sue had so carefully researched.

Now, I went back and reviewed the workbooks that I had accumulated over the years. I felt as if I were starting at the beginning again, learning to re-weave the tapestry anew, to put the pieces back together into a pattern of perfect alignment. But I wasn't at all sure how to begin.

At about this time, I came across a book while browsing in a local bookstore that was to change my life. It expanded my understanding of who we really are, and allowed me to put the trauma that I had experienced from the loss of my child into a new perspective. I remembered Sue's advice to start at the top and work down, and so it was that I was guided to read *Oneness*, received and transcribed by Rasha. This book was a revelation for me, giving me the clarity of spiritual understanding that I had lacked previously. I found it to be intensely personal, as if it were written only for me. Yet it was universal in its portrayal of the human condition.

It was not easy reading. There was much that I couldn't absorb at first. But I reread it and reread it again, lingering over each paragraph. Over the next year, I read this book at least five times, cover-to-cover, all four hundred and two pages, until the concepts of transformation and soul evolution finally made sense to me.

I read, "It is here, in the heart-centered core of your being, that the timeless connections with the multidimensional aspects of self will be made manifest. And it is here that you will encounter the gateway to unification with the Oneness that you are. The question is, are you willing to risk relinquishing all that you know—the entire structure of the belief system that defines and constricts your reality—for the chance that you may experience the perspective of your own expanded Self? You stand at the threshold of a grand adventure." [4]

I read about integrating fragmented aspects of consciousness, and about the need to release cellular imprinting. I read about peeling back layers of emotional density. I read about confronting resistance to change and overcoming karmic conditioning. I read about the significance of energy work and the purpose of the journey into humanness and duality. [5]

And I read about allowing others to live or to die in freedom. "The lesson for you in such dramas is to let go of your attachment to the physical life of another, and to know that life, in the higher sense, transcends the identity that may be choosing to relinquish form. To confront death and perceive it as the portal that it truly is, enables you to transcend the limitation of attachment to form, and to grasp the eternal wisdom that is possible in the act of letting go. Longevity is not the objective of a physical incarnation, but rather, it is the fulfillment of one's life purpose." [6]

ᥫᩰ

I studied these concepts at length until I could relate to them in an experiential way. It was not enough to understand them intellectually; I needed to experience them. And little by little, it dawned on me that

I knew these profound spiritual concepts intimately. They would become the foundation of my core beliefs.

During this time of intense study, I still suffered from physical complaints. I couldn't shake off the chronic stress that I had lived with for so long. It had become a constant presence in my life. I rarely enjoyed a full night's sleep. In fact, there were many days when I went to work after having had only three or four hours of restorative sleep the previous night. And the allergies that I had developed were interfering with my ability to function, both at work and at home.

In *Oneness* it is written that the basis for virtually all physical health conditions is energy related. "True healing occurs when one has succeeded in releasing the underlying vibrational charge one has carried at certain levels of awareness." [7]

Modern physicists study how matter and energy interact in the visible and the invisible worlds. Everything is vibration, including our thoughts, feelings, and emotions. And everything is interrelated. What elicits change in one part affects the whole. Nothing stands in isolation.

I believe that my allergies were the physical manifestation of the fear and insecurity that was still a major part of my outlook on life. I was hypervigilant to perceived dangers, and as a result, my body was continuously overreacting to all manner of common substances found in the natural world. I underwent testing and was found to be reactive to multiple indoor and outdoor year-round allergens. So I decided on a course of weekly desensitizing shots to help my body slowly recover from its hypervigilance.

But the worst was yet to come. After more than a year of weekly allergy shots, I was much improved, but the prolonged experience of allergic symptoms had left me unable to breathe through my nose without daily decongestant medications. I simply couldn't accept that I would have to take medicine for the rest of my life just to breathe. I wanted to breathe freely! So after careful thought, I made the decision to undergo nasal surgery to trim overgrown tissue and bone, and to straighten my septum.

Over the holidays of the third Christmas after Kate's death, I scheduled this elective surgery. All went well, the surgery was successful, and my recovery was progressing, until shortly after I finished my course of preventive antibiotics. The very drugs that were supposed to prevent postoperative infection ironically made me vulnerable to one of the "super bugs" so commonly found now in hospitals and outpatient surgical centers: Clostridium difficile.

I had succumbed to a horrendous C-diff infection. This bacteria kills people! In the last few years, C-diff has become highly virulent. It now produces about twenty times more toxins than it did just a few years ago. I became very ill.

After years of unrelenting struggle, both in the last years of Kate's life and in the three years since her death, my body had finally broken down.

Fortunately, my brother and sister, both physicians, had alerted me to the possibility of a C-diff infection, and I was able to be treated quickly. But I continued to have extreme pain and overwhelming fatigue for many months. I managed to continue working, but I could do little else. I was barely surviving one day at a time. My symptoms were so extreme that I wondered if my infection could have triggered full blown fibromyalgia. My doctor didn't know how to help me. I was discouraged, disheartened, and on my own.

There were many times in the three years since Kate's death when I thought that I had hit bottom. But I was wrong. Marian had said that if you're falling down an elevator shaft, you can't do anything until you hit bottom. Then, she said, you can choose to lie there, or you can decide to crawl back out and reclaim your life. I wanted to reclaim my life. I desperately wanted my good health back. I wanted the abundant physical vitality of my youth. So I studied the latest research on fibromyalgia and its coexisting conditions. I ordered all variety of supplements that promised relief from the pain and stiffness I experienced every day, but nothing helped. I couldn't focus on anything except my pain.

PART THREE

HOME AGAIN

I.

And so it was in this condition that I found myself six months later walking the Kabbalah trails at Sue Gurnee's workshop at Growing Wheel International. I had not been to a workshop in over three years, but now I was excited to be in the presence of like-minded people committed to their own personal development through energetic awareness. Every workshop that I've ever attended with Sue has been life-altering in some way. This workshop became the steady climb from the bottom of the elevator shaft into the light of a new life. It proved to be the turning point in my recovery. But more than that, my intense desire to reach the Crown and the subsequent feeling of incredible joy, also became my pilgrimage "up the mountain" to a higher level of awareness. It was an experience so profound, so sublime in its perfection, that I knew I was forever changed.

From my previous work, I knew that everything vibrates at a specific frequency. To change patterns of vibration requires an awareness of the underlying areas of dysfunction. I soon realized that the cells of our body hold the vibrational memory of previous trauma, illness, and injury. In order to heal myself, I had to energetically release the body memories that I still held of the shock, devastation, and trauma I had experienced at Kate's death. I had to connect with the pure energy of the earth and reclaim the optimal function of my physical systems. I had much work to do.

I returned home and renewed my study of the chakra system. I now had a renewed sense of clarity that had previously eluded me. I found a wonderful book written by Anodea Judith, a pioneer in introducing the chakra system within the context of western psychology. *Eastern Body, Western Mind: Psychology and the Chakra System as a Path to the Self* gave me a deeper understanding, a new approach, to the self-purification inherent in walking the Rainbow Path that Marian had spoken of. I looked more deeply into my fears of the physical world. The recurring dreams of a lion loose in the house had continued, and I knew that I had to address my feelings of safety and my sense of security in the world.

Memories reside in a timeless place: *I see myself as a young child, perhaps three or four years of age. I am playing outside after dinner one evening with my sister and a few neighborhood playmates. We are active children in the 1950s, and many of the families in our neighborhood enjoy sitting outside and socializing on warm summer evenings. On this summer evening, my friends and I find ourselves sitting on the porch of a neighbor several doors down. We*

are listening to this neighbor as he tells us that our govern-
ment's testing of atomic bombs will bring destruction upon
us all. I see myself, wide-eyed, as this man explains to us
that if we keep setting off atomic bombs, the dinosaurs that
are asleep in the ocean are going to reawaken and take over
the world. My young, innocent self is terrified, and soon I
am running home, all sense of safety shattered. For many
months, I worry about these dinosaurs. I fear going to sleep
because I know that a dinosaur will stick his head in my
window and devour me. But I am a creative child. Soon I
have invented an invisible playmate, a good dinosaur, a
plant-eating brontosaurus that will protect me from the ty-
rannosaurus rex that lives across the street. I see myself lying
down for my afternoon nap, nodding off in the company of
my pet dinosaur.

As I grew up, these seeds of fear and insecurity
remained tucked away, hidden from conscious awareness. I now know that the tactic of finding safety outside of the self, as I did as a child, does not serve me as
an adult. I needed to release these residual false fears
and find my comfort in the manifest world.

I remember visiting my brother in Colorado a few
years ago. We were driving through the Thompson
River Valley on our way to Estes Park. On either side
of the roadway soared huge rock cliffs many hundreds
of feet up to the sky. I was in awe of the majesty of
the forces that formed our earth. I was in awe of the
power and the beauty of the Rocky Mountains. I now
recalled this feeling to envelope myself in the strength

and stability of Mother Earth. I visualized sending the vibrant red energy of my first chakra deep into the heart of the Mother, and I finally felt safe, secure, and supported.

Thoughts create our reality. I worked in spheres of awareness as Sue had taught me, to gracefully release conflicts and replace them with the new patterns that I wished to establish. I worked with each of the energy centers of the chakra system, consciously recalling scenes from my life that had formed the foundation of my personality. I arranged for personal sessions with Sue to help me find these areas of dysfunction and energetic density, and to clear and reprogram them.

From *Oneness*, I read, "By being totally authentic in your humanness—your human frailties as well as your strengths, your perceived shortcomings as well as your triumphs, your darkest hour as well as your shining moments—you set the stage for becoming the shining example of triumph over adversity that you truly are."[8]

ভ

From Anodea Judith's book, I learned that the second chakra energy relates to the fluid realm of our emotions and involves our basic right to feel these emotions. It also addresses the issue of our ability to experience genuine pleasure. The third chakra, the fiery center of our personal power and will, relates to the ability to act from our own sense of inner authority. The fourth chakra, our heart center, involves our right to love and be loved. The fifth chakra energy represents our ability to speak and hear our own truth. The sixth chakra relates to the capacity to see and trust in our own perceptions. And the seventh chakra connects us with our own spiritual truths.[9]

My work in these areas was very intense, but I was highly motivated. I wanted to regain my optimal health. I wanted to be as free and easy in my physicality as I was as a child, when I would glide over the ice on my skates, slicing through the still air of a freezing Minnesota winter.

Memories reside in a timeless place: *I am nine years old and we live in St. Paul across the street from an outdoor skating rink. I see myself eagerly racing across the street every afternoon to join the other children in their joyful exuberance. I am impervious to the frigid air as I bend down to lace up my skates while exhaling puffs of cloudy white breath in the bright light of day. Effortlessly, I slide across the ice; forwards, backwards, swaying, circling. If I fall, I get back up, laughing, and take off again with no thought of injury or pain. For hours after school each day, I revel in the freedom of movement until it gets dark and it is time to go home to a warm dinner.*

This is how I want to be - fully expressive, effortless, free, and fearless. I visualized this image often, knowing that I was tapping the healing power of focused intent.

In the months following my experience in the mountains, I began reading about the Kabbalah. While most commonly associated with the Jewish faith, Kabbalah is actually a systematic overview of the wisdom teachings underlying many spiritual traditions, including Christianity. The study of Kabbalah is the study of the nature of God, the created universe, and our own unique place within this created universe. It utilizes a symbolic diagram called The Tree of Life to organize ten characteristics, or emanations, of God. These ten channels of Divine emanations are referred to as the ten sefirot. The organization of The Tree of Life can resemble the human body; the ten sefirot representing particular areas of the body and the corresponding energetic centers, or major chakras.

I found Kabbalah to be fascinating, complex, challenging, and comprehensive. It is a system that when conscientiously understood, allows us to integrate our mind and emotions to align with the spiritual energies that are the foundation of all life. It is a lifelong pursuit to understand the subtleties and progressive levels of enlightenment that Kabbalah offers.

I also studied homeopathy, which is an energetic healing modality founded upon the Law of Similars. Remedies which hold minute frequencies of individual plants, minerals, or animal substances, are taken which treat the body/mind as a whole unit and stimulate healing on multiple levels. Additionally, I used essential oils for relaxation and to support the immune system, and various flower essences to address fundamental issues.

While I certainly do not claim to be especially adept at any of these healing methods, I learned enough to help myself on my path of recovery.

II.

Slowly over the next few months, my physical health improved. Though I still experienced some pain and stiffness, I was miles ahead of where I was after my surgery. I continued to explore various supplements that would strengthen my immune system and release inflammation, and I worked constantly to establish the perfect pattern of action and reaction in the nervous system. Throughout these many months, I would occasionally make contact with Kate, but I found more and more that I could feel her presence in my own heart's love for her. And I would know that all was well.

After our workshop with Sue, I felt compelled to visit Marian once again. I found her as always, seemingly ageless, as if the passing years had had no effect on her at all. Kate's beautiful angel statue stood in the garden, a permanent fixture at Terra Nova Center.

Again, we started with a short prayer as we sat down facing each other. Marian then said, "Kate is alive, well, and ecstatically happy. She doesn't know loneliness; she doesn't know grief. She is so busy where she is, but it's all in loving service. She has gone up and she is still climbing the mountain. She is dragging no chains of judgment or grief or anger or fear. She is just radiant Light. If you could think of the most beautiful angel that you can imagine, that is Kate now."

When I told Marian that I could feel Kate's presence in my heart, she said, "That is because she is part of your soul pattern. When you talk to her in the memory banks that are within you, you hear her voice of many lifetimes. The healing has been accomplished. Your way is clear now."

III.

Later, when I had returned home, in meditation I asked, "Kate, are you my angel now?"

She replied:

> *I am Freedom, I am Light,*
> *I am the brilliant glitter of the starry night.*
> *I am your daughter, I am your mother.*
> *I am your student, I am your teacher.*
> *I am the love in our deepest hearts*
> *That is great beyond measure.*

I simply cannot express the joy that I felt on hearing these words. We both laughed, and I was grateful for this most wondrous gift that I had received. Marian was right, I did feel a lightness, a lifting of the heavy grief that I had carried for more than three years.

But this story is not yet complete, for the recognition that profound grief can be a catalyst for great spiritual awakening was slowly becoming apparent to me. Over the next several months, I paid attention to my dreams. I paid attention to the sensations in my body. Sometimes it seemed that I would take three steps forward and two steps back. Some days I would feel enthusiastic and energetic, and other days I'd feel discouraged. But I never lost confidence that I was slowly making progress in my goal of optimal health and vitality. My pain was lessening, and I found a new doctor who listened to my concerns and helped me with my chronic sleep problems. I discovered that a good night's sleep helped my body repair the stresses that it had endured. And I took a brief period of time every day to meditate and pray. Sometimes insights would come to me during the night or first thing in the morning. I always kept a pencil and paper by the bed. One morning I had a vision.

I awaken early, well before dawn. As I lay still in the darkness, I see a figure of brilliant, blazing, silvery light. Bright and radiant, how beautiful she is! Instinctively I know that she is a manifestation of my purest Self. I feel this exalted vibration within my physical body. It is a subtle hum that energizes and enlivens every atom, cell, organ, gland, tissue, and fiber of my body. It penetrates all the way to the quantum level, and I feel a wholeness that I've never experienced before. It is the marriage of the physical with the timeless essence of all life. Without question, I know that I am a Strayaway Child no longer, for I have found my way Home.

ൟ

Slowly over time, my concept of who I am has shifted. From an expanded vista, I can objectively observe myself as the personality of Anne, the end result of all the events experienced and habits developed over the years. I see all of the struggles and worries that I've endured. I see how reactions to the world around me have become automatic over the course of time, and I see how this has restricted me. Now, more than ever, I am determined to objectively release the patterns that no longer serve me, with love, compassion and understanding.

IV.

Today is my fifty-seventh birthday. On this day, I realize that for all of these years, my body has been my most loyal friend. Scenes from my life scroll through my mind, and I see a young child hopping fences, climbing trees, and running like the wind. I see her as she experiences untold numbers of bumps and scrapes. I see her as she succumbs to illness and yet recovers time and time again. Sometimes with the help of modern medicine, sometimes in nature's own miraculous way.

My body has seen me through awkward adolescence, followed by the blossoming of young womanhood. It has carried and safely delivered two babies. To bring new life into the world is surely marvelous and miraculous!

It has carried me into the middle years. It has suffered pain, anxiety, exhaustion, poor diet, lack of sleep and exercise. And still it has recovered to carry me yet further along this road of life.

It has survived the shock and trauma of a child's death. And yet again, it has recovered, if much more slowly than from any previous assault to its senses.

Now my body has entered a new phase, unencumbered by the repeating cycles of hormonal fluctuations.

I look at my face in the mirror and see lines developing around my eyes. My skin, though still soft, is much less firm than in youth. But I am not discouraged, I am in awe!

I am just now learning how to honor this body and its unique sensitivities, and to care for it as my dearest friend, confident in its support for the many years of service yet to come.

∾

Days passed into weeks. Soon I had another vision.

I am sitting on the steps that lead to my backyard. It is a comfortable October night and the moon is almost full. I look up at the trees, dark against the background of fluffy clouds in the night sky. I hear crickets chirping and traffic noises. I focus on the natural night sounds of the insects. I look up and notice that the moon has cast a soft light over everything. The clouds seem illuminated against the darker blue of the sky. Within seconds I notice a shift, a new vibration. The outer world recedes and I am enveloped in absolute peace. I feel ageless vitality and expansive perfect stillness. I feel alive with the vibrancy of life. I have no struggles, no worries. I feel free. I feel joyful! Is this a vision of heaven and earth and man and all creatures living and breathing and being in perfect harmony? The New Garden of Eden? A New Earth?

I later wondered if I could wake up every day in this place of "no-struggle". What if I could hold this frequency every day, throughout the day, as I go about my activities, my work, my play, my interactions with others? I determined to practice and focus and retrieve this feeling over and over again, until it is my touchstone, my foundation, my new way of being.

V.

The fourth Christmas season since Kate's passing was uneventful. I felt relieved of the awful grief that had plagued me at previous celebrations, and I found that I could enjoy the simple festivities of the season. For in my heart of hearts, I felt Kate's presence. She was always with me. We were united by the love between our two souls, as we journeyed together in this present life and beyond. For truly, there are no boundaries that can contain the fullness and the expansiveness of love. While we look with wonder and awe on the tangible manifestations of our material existence, the mountains and seas, the sun, moon, stars, and planets, the greatest mystery of all is the expansion of Divine Intelligence into an awareness of Self which we identify as our soul. This is truly the pulse of the Creative Force, greater than our human minds can comprehend. But in our hearts, we feel this immeasurable power, the mystery of love. Love is the substance of the Divine. Love is the matrix of worlds upon worlds and universes upon universes. And when we love one another completely, unconditionally, and unreservedly, we are aligned with our own Divine nature. We are one with all.

Shortly after the holidays, we had our first significant snowfall in several years. I had forgotten how beautiful the snow can be as it drifts out of the sky and settles in a sparkly blanket over the ground. I took my dog, Buzz, out into the backyard to watch him explore the fluffy white stuff, and I began to think of the approaching fourth anniversary of Kate's passing. I made plans to buy a new flower arrangement to put on her gravesite, for I like to change the colors every season. I usually visit her grave every week or two just to make sure all is well. I know she is not there, but I like to look at all of the colorful flowers dotting the rolling hills. There are no headstones in this section of the cemetery, only flowers, and I find this place to be peaceful, quiet and lovingly tended. Consecrated ground. I decided on white roses this time.

I was preoccupied with these thoughts as Buzz and I came in from the cold, and when I stepped into the house, a very odd thing happened. When I lifted my left foot to kick the snow off of my shoe, my supporting right leg locked and I started to lose my balance. With a sense of unreality, I found myself falling. I couldn't catch myself. I was going down! As I hit the floor hard, I felt a very sharp pain just below my right knee. I lay on the floor for several minutes, running my hands over the painful area, unable to get up. When I finally tried to stand, I found that I was unable to put any weight on my leg. I called out to Will, and he helped me hobble over to the recliner. I was in tremendous pain as I elevated my leg, and Will got me an ice pack from the freezer. Once again, I was dependent on his care and support, for I had broken my leg!

❧

For the next eight weeks, I lived in my recliner, unable even to go up the stairs to my bed. Will cared for me so very attentively, preparing my food, shopping for groceries, and driving me to my doctor's appointments. I was completely dependent in a way that I had never before experienced, and I slowly realized that I had to thoroughly surrender to this process. I didn't understand why this had happened, but I was in a unique position to learn the lesson of total surrender and trust.

I was forced to ask myself this question: Do I really have perfect trust? Do I embody the perfect trust shown by the storm-lashed sailor as he rides the choppy waters of the deep sea on a black night? No starlight penetrates the roiling clouds to guide his way as he is buffeted by salt spray and cowers in fear of the howling winds. The sailor's only choice is to trust that his compass is true and that it will guide him to maintain course while he sails into the calm dawn. Have I learned this perfect trust? Trust that there is a reason for all that happens in our lives? Trust that there is a guiding force at work, and that there is a purpose for events that challenge us? Total and complete surrender to my own purest transcendent Self was the missing element that I had yet to realize in my evolution through recovery.

Since I was unable to go to work, I began to look upon this time as an unexpected sabbatical from daily responsibilities. I had plenty of time to reflect, and I vowed to take better care of myself. I vowed to improve my diet and take an interest in cooking foods that support my body's efforts to heal. I vowed to start exercising when my broken leg was strong again. But complete surrender came hard for me, and within two weeks, everything on my right side hurt. Once again, my nervous system was overloaded, and once again the chicken pox virus from my childhood was reactivated and I developed shingles.

I had to take strong medicine for the pain, and my body lay anesthetized while I slowly recovered. I slept, I dreamed.

I am at the seashore. There are people all around me, and buildings, and the bustle of everyday activity. The sky is clear, cerulean blue and the air feels warm on my face. I look out at the ocean and see small waves breaking on the shore line. All seems calm out in the deep water, but somehow instinctively, I know a tsunami is coming. I try to warn people but no one believes me! I am looking for Will to alert him, and when I find him with his friends, even he says I must be overreacting. Soon the water is surging toward us and Will and I start running. Now everyone around us is running from the approaching waves. We must climb to higher ground! We come across an old empty building, and Will and I race up the steps to the entrance. The water is rushing in, unrelenting, unstoppable. More people are becoming aware of what is happening and try to escape, but still they underestimate the severity of the situation. The water roars as it continues rising. The sound is overwhelming! A second seems eternal, a freeze-frame of no-time. Surely the water must be cresting soon. Up and up we go until we find a small stairway leading to the roof of the old building. As we try to outrun the water, I worry that the force of the waves will collapse the wooden supports under us. Still, the water rises. We have almost reached the top most attic space, and the only way out is to break through the wooden frame and roof shingles overhead. Once through, we can go no higher. We stand at the highest point of all the surrounding area. From this vantage, I see that the water has swallowed all but where we are standing. But now as I look around me, I notice that the sea has calmed, and a sense of hushed quiet envelops the scene. The surface of the water reflects the golden radiance of a new dawn. Everything is changed, everything is incredibly peaceful, and I sense the power and majesty of a Force that cannot be adequately described.

I awoke from this dream shaken, still at the mercy of a process I didn't even yet fully understand.

ᐤ

Soon, the empty hours of the day, day after day sitting in my recliner, pressed upon me. I found the deep quiet to be alive with a faint pulse somewhat like crickets chirping. I've always found the process of creative endeavors to be relaxing and enjoyable, and so in the quiet hours I began to string gemstone beads into necklaces. Rose quartz, citrine, amethyst, topaz, apatite, tourmaline, and garnet, I worked with all varieties of earth stones. I even broke down old necklaces to restring. Many of these necklaces I gave to friends and relatives, for it was in the handling of the stones that I found pleasure. And in this way, I passed the days, staying focused in the present moment.

During this time, I noticed that occasionally my legs would jerk unexpectedly, a surprising and odd sensation outside of my conscious control. I decided to review my collection of books on energetics for any reference to this strange sensation and I came across the term *kriyas*, the Sanskrit name given to these involuntary body movements. They can be likened to the thrashing movements of a coiled or kinked garden hose as water flows through it. In the physical body, the primal cosmic energy, also called prana (Sanskrit for "vital life"), flows through a particular area resulting in a sensation of electricity passing through the nerves. Kriyas are associated with the phenomenon of kundalini. And so my research into this little understood process began.

I discovered that the study of the kundalini phe-
nomenom originates in the ancient yogic traditions
of India. In broad terms, it refers to spiritual energy
driving the evolutionary process in mankind toward
an expanded level of consciousness. Ordinarily, this
energy lies dormant at the base of the spine, but when
activated, either through spiritual discipline, a crisis,
a strong desire to understand the meaning of life, or
specifically focused energetic work, this potent life-
force energy begins the ascent up the spinal column,
ultimately reaching and activating a portion of the
brain. Kundalini is a catalyst for physiological change
based on spiritual evolution. This primal component
of the bio-electromagnetic energy flowing through the
body results in various, unique, and at times unpleas-
ant sensations as it refines the physical system for a
higher level of consciousness.

I realized that many of the physical symptoms that
I had experienced were actually the result of a poorly
understood and undirected flow of this potent energy
throughout my body. The pain and stiffness, the in-
terrupted sleep patterns, the involuntary jerking, the
sensitive digestive and nervous systems, even the expansion of psychic phenomenon, I discovered all to
be symptomatic of the kundalini energy active over
many years. I found much of the vocabulary describing this evolutionary transformation to be foreign to
my Western ear, but I understood and could visualize
the concepts clearly.

The man most credited with introducing the modern model of an awakened kundalini to the Western world was Gopi Krishna (1903–1984). Born in relative poverty in Kashmir, by profession he was a modest Indian civil servant concerned with the day-to-day tasks of providing for his family. In all outward appearances, he was quite ordinary. However, in his autobiography *Living with Kundalini*, he relates his personal experience of an expanded awakening, initiated by an ecstatic vision which he described as infinite transcendent awareness. This extraordinary event occurred during his usual daily meditation at the age of thirty-four. For the next twelve years, he struggled to understand, harmonize, and direct this force, and in the process, suffered great physical, emotional, and psychic symptoms.

He studied the ancient yogic texts to find references for this type of experience, in particular hoping to find information regarding the physiological implications of transcendent awareness. He believed that mystical experiences such as the saints and seers throughout history have reported, represent only the beginning levels of a transformational consciousness. It was his greatest hope that scientific research into the interrelationship between brain physiology and consciousness would eventually corroborate the kundalini force as the evolutionary process in man.

In his autobiography, he beautifully and eloquently describes prana as "the life energy by which divinity brings into existence the organic kingdoms and acts on the organic structures...while remaining constant and unaltered fundamentally, acting as both the architect and the object produced. It exists as a mighty universe, vaster and more wonderful than the cosmos perceived by our senses, with its own spheres and planes, corresponding to the suns and earths, its own materials and bricks, its own movement and inertia, its own light and shadow, laws and properties, existing side-by-side with the universe we see, interwoven with our thoughts and actions, interpenetrating the atoms and molecules of matter, radiating with light, moving with wind and tide, marvelously subtle and agile, the stuff of our fancies and dreams, the life principle of creation which is woven inextricably with the very texture of our being."[10]

Gopi Krishna remained a humble and ordinary man all of his life, living simply and endeavoring to bring to the world an understanding of the transformation of consciousness that he believed all are destined to eventually experience.

୧୨

I now had the information I needed to organize my experiences into context within the bigger picture.

In meditation, I visualized this fine life force energy traveling up the proper pathway, the central canal of the subtle body, the sushumna in Eastern terminology, just as I had walked up the central pillar of the Kabbalah trails to the Crown. In time, with consistent focused intent and attention to diet and exercise, my broken leg healed quickly and completely and I felt much relief from the muscular tension and pain that had plagued me for so long. I also realized that to balance the accelerated pace of modern living, rest and quiet time are vitally important. I soon found that I had the energy to resume my normal activities with a new-found confidence in my ability to ride the waves and currents of life's uncertainties.

VI.

My journey through and recovery from the profound grief of the loss of my child has taken much longer than I could have imagined on the day that I received the awful news of Kate's death. Though the characteristics of grieving are common to all, everyone's experience is unique. God has gifted us with multiple cultural and spiritual traditions with which to heal and transcend our most crippling pain. I began my journey with the desire to find my child, to discover where she had gone after she left this earth plane. Jesus said, "For where your treasure is, there will your heart be also."[11]

I was compelled to stretch beyond this everyday life of work, social responsibilities, and conventional ideas. I was driven to follow Kate into the spiritual realm. But as I progressed in my greater understanding of this other reality, my journey then became one of personal discovery. It became a sacred quest, the quest of the Strayaway Child. I found answers to the bigger question of who we really are. I found the multidimensional aspects of Self that Rasha has written about in *Oneness*.

My experience of profound grief has been both the worst and the greatest experience of my life. I now feel incredible gratitude, for I know that I have grown into a deeper understanding of my true Self. And I know without doubt that there is a much greater power at work in our lives.

Undoubtedly, there will be times in the future when I may feel deep sadness. Sometimes even now, tears come unbidden to my eyes when I think of how Kate would drape her little child's body around mine as if we were one organism. I miss the everyday physical interaction, going to a movie or luncheon in a restaurant. Perhaps on Kate's birthday, I may say, "She would have been twenty-eight years old today." Or I'll wonder what her life might have been like when she would have been thirty or forty years old. But I am comforted beyond what I can express to hear her voice in my head saying, "Hi, Mom!" and to know beyond all doubt that she is brilliantly alive.

EPILOGUE

Once again I am climbing upward on the Kabbalah trails in the Appalachian Mountains. It has been two years since I first visited the Crown, and more than five years since Kate left this earth and passed into the spiritual world. This beautiful, bright summer day in June is far removed from the cold drizzle of an overcast February day in 2006. Today, I want to hear birdsong and feel the heat of the sun on my face and the soft wind in my hair. I want to sit in quiet contemplation in this heaven on earth amidst the rocks and trees and rich soil. I want to immerse myself within the vibrations of the first sefirah again.

On this day, I have the mountain all to myself. A thought flashes through my mind for a few, brief seconds: *If I fall, if I lie here alone and injured, no one will know.* I stand my ground and stare fear full in the face. I have come too far to let fear get the best of me.

Onward I go. As before, I plot my course from tree to tree, breaking this journey down into small victories of just three or four feet at a time. I cling to the trunks of the tall pines as I slowly make my way upward, pausing often to breathe deeply and sip from my water bottle. In this way, the first hour crawls by.

Farther up the trail, I catch a glimpse of the fallen trees where I had rested on my first ascent so long ago. On that day, Will told me, "Once you pass this group of fallen trees, the path isn't as steep." But the last push to the top seems much steeper than I remember.

Sometime in the two years since I was here last, logs have been placed strategically to assist climbers as they navigate the final part of the path. In the steepest section, I sit on these logs and push off with my legs, scooting upward in a backward motion. I am determined to reach the Crown in whatever manner is necessary, and before long, I am able to stand upright again. Thirty minutes later, I approach the rocks signifying that I have reached the Crown, the first sefirah of the Kabbalah and the frequency of the Divine infinite and unmanifest potential. It was on these rocks that I had lain so weak and exhausted on my first visit here.

Today, I sit on these same rocks and quietly think of the perfection of the moment. I sit in silence, drinking in the sunlight sifting through the trees in glowing beams of light, ever changing. I think of recent events, recent challenges, and recent losses. I think of my mother's passing just three months ago, and how, at the end of her long, drawn out illness, the memory that I pulled from the timeless place is that of my own young self waving goodbye and blowing her a kiss every morning as I climbed aboard the school bus in front of our house to go to kindergarten. For in the end, there is only love.

I breathe in the sweetness of this summer morning, and acknowledge how perfectly safe I feel, all alone on top of this mountain. For it is in solitary intimacy with our Divine nature that we find our way purposefully through this life of uncertainty.

After a time, I notice an orange tie on a tree a short distance away in the direction of the ridgeline. I walk toward it and decide to continue on this course, for I believe it will lead me down a gentler descent from the top. I walk beyond the tree with the orange tie and shortly I see another orange spot visible through the low-lying branches and dense shrubbery. Eagerly I continue, finding the marked path through the woods. It is a magical scene as I slowly make my way through this sacred place. Suddenly in the distance, an animal crashes through the brush and runs at full speed away from me. To my surprise, I see that it is a coyote, but I feel no fear, only a deep, abiding peace all around me.

The unexpected presence of the coyote reminds me that life presents us with surprises from time to time. Like the patterns of sunlight as it plays with the leaves that dance gracefully in the whispering wind above me, life is never static. Occasionally, life's surprises present us with loss. But no matter what form this loss takes, whether it be the loss of a loved one, the loss of a job, loss of possessions or relationships, the loss of good health, or even the loss of our illusions, what cannot be lost is the Spirit within us. And our Spirit is like the warm rays of the sun that nurture the budding seed. It is far greater than we can know. It is everlasting and powerful enough to heal the deepest wounds of a broken heart.

And so, with a light step, I make my way down the mountain, knowing with perfect trust that the path is true.

Katherine Jeanne Hess

1984–2006

AUTHOR'S NOTE

"The Strayaway Child" is a traditional six-part Irish jig attributed to Margaret Barry and Michael Gorman.

Margaret Barry (1917–1989) was a ballad singer and street musician from Cork City. She came from a musical family of travelers but left home at the age of fourteen after a family disagreement following the death of her mother. In the Alan Lomax *Portraits Collection*, Margaret recounts how the tune of the jig came to her in a dream. But it was left to her musical collaborator, the Sligo fiddler Michael Gorman (1896–1970), to organize and arrange the parts into what is now recognized as the traditional jig.

Over the years, many artists have recorded "The Strayaway Child," most notably The Bothy Band on the CD *Out of the Wind, Into the Sun* from 1977, on which the tune is titled "The Strayaway Girl."

However, it was the grand masters of traditional Irish music, The Chieftains, who, under the direction of founding member Paddy Moloney, created a new interpretation of this traditional tune. By slowing the tempo, adding the steady beat of the bodhran (the traditional Irish goatskin drum), and employing the earthy drone of the didgeridoo, "The Strayaway

Child" has now become a sorrowful lament. It has now become a dirge. It is a masterful interpretation, visceral in its effect on the listener. In my mind, this version of "The Strayaway Child" is the perfect expression of the grief of profound loss.

"The Strayaway Child," recorded by the Chieftains, can be heard on the CD *A Chieftains Celebration* from 1989.

For those who wish to explore the world of energetic principles to enhance self-awareness, I refer the reader to www.suegurnee.com. And Reverend Marian Starnes may be contacted through her website at www.terranovacenter.com.

The book *Oneness* may be purchased through www.onenesswebsite.com or through www.Amazon.com. *Eastern Body, Western Mind: Psychology and the Chakra System as a Path to the Self*, as well as *Living with Kundalini: The Autobiography of Gopi Krishna* may also be purchased through www.Amazon.com. An in-depth explanation of the kundalini phenomenon can be found on the website www.biologyofkundalini.com.

END NOTES

[1] Anodea Judith, *Eastern Body, Western Mind: Psychology and the Chakra System as a Path to the Self* (Celestial Arts, 2004) 2.

[2] *The Holy Bible, Red Letter Edition, King James Version* (Books, Inc., Publishers) Genesis 9:12-15.

[3] Stephen Venables, *Everest, Summit of Achievement* (Simon & Schuster, 2003) 62.

[4] Rasha, *Oneness* (Earthstar Press, 2003) 38, 22.

[5] Rasha, Contents.

[6] Rasha, 173, 391.

[7] Rasha, 289, 298.

[8] Rasha, 97.

[9] Anodea Judith, 26-28.

[10] Gopi Krishna, *Living with Kundalini, The Autobiography of Gopi Krishna* (Shambhala Publications, Inc., 1993) 199-200.

[11] *The Holy Bible,* Matthew 6:21.

BIBLIOGRAPHY

Amen, Daniel G., MD. *Healing ADD, The Breakthrough Program that Allows You to See and Heal the 6 Types of ADD.* New York, NY. The Berkeley Publishing Group. 2001.

Bailey, Philip M., MD. *Homeopathic Psychology: Personality Profiles of the Major Constitutional Remedies.* Berkeley, CA. North Atlantic Books. 1995.

Bonner, John. *Qabalah: A Magical Primer.* Boston MA/ York Beach, ME. Weiser Books. 2002.

Breggin, Peter R., MD. *Brain Disabling Treatments in Psychiatry, Drugs, Electroshock, and the Psychopharmaceutical Complex. Second Edition.* New York, NY. Springer Publishing Company. 2008.

---. *Medication Madness: The Role of Psychiatric Drugs in Cases of Violence, Suicide, and Crime.* New York, NY. St. Martin's Press. 2008.

Chappell, Peter. *Emotional Healing with Homeopathy: Treating the Effects of Trauma.* Berkeley, CA. North Atlantic Books. 2003.

Gurnee, Susan. *Longing for Change: Inner Studies Series Workbook*. Growing Wheel International. Susan Gurnee, 1st. Books. 2003.

Hershoff, Asa, ND. *Homeopathic Remedies*. New York. Avery, Penguin Putnam. 2000.

Horacek, H. Joseph, Jr. *Brainstorms: Understanding and Treating the Emotional Storms of Attention Deficit Hyperactivity Disorder from Childhood through Adulthood*. Northvale, NJ, London. Jason Aronson, Inc. 1998.

Judith, Anodea. *Eastern Body, Western Mind: Psychology and the Chakra System as a Path to the Self*. Berkeley. Celestial Arts. 2004.

---. *Wheels of Life: A User's Guide to the Chakra System*. St. Paul, MN. Llewellyn. 1995.

Kaminski, Patricia, and Richard Katz. *Flower Essence Repertory: A Comprehensive Guide to North American and English Flower Essences for Emotional and Spiritual Well-Being*. Nevada City, CA. The Flower Essence Society. 1994.

Kason, Yvonne, MD. *Farther Shores: Exploring How Near-Death, Kundalini, and Mystical Experiences Can Transform Ordinary Lives*. Bloomington, IN. iUniverse. 1994. 2000. 2008.

Keiffer, Gene. *Kundalini, Empowering Human Evolution: Selected Writings of Gopi Krishna*. New York, NY. Paragon House. 1996.

Khalsa, Gurmukh Kaur, and Andrew Newberg, Savananda Radha, Ken Wilber, John Selby. *Kundalini Rising: Exploring the Energy of Awakening.* Boulder, CO. Sounds True, Inc. 2009.

Krishna, Gopi. *Living with Kundalini: The Autobiography of Gopi Krishna.* Boston, MA. Shambhala Publications, Inc. 1993.

---. *Higher Consciousness and Kundalini.* ON, Canada. F.I.N.D Research Trust, Institute for Consciousness Research. 1974.

Kumar, Ravindra, PhD, and Jytte Kumar Larson. *The Kundalini Book of Living and Dying: Gateways to Higher Consciousness.* Boston, MA/York Beach, ME. Weiser Books. 2004.

Laitman, Rav Michael. *The Complete Idiot's Guide to Kabbalah.* New York. Alpha, Penguin Group. 2007.

Pearce, Joseph Chilton. *The Biology of Transcendence: A Blueprint of the Human Spirit.* Rochester, VT. Park Street Press. 2002.

Peirce, Penney. *Frequency: The Power of Personal Vibration.* New York, NY. Simon and Schuster, Inc. 2009.

Prophet, Elizabeth Clare. *Kabbalah: Key to Your Inner Power.* Livingston, MT. Summit University Press. 1997.

---, and Patricia Spadaro. *Your Seven Energy Centers: A Holistic Approach to Physical, Emotional, and Spiritual Vitality*. Gardiner, Mt. Summit University Press. 2000.

Rasha. *Oneness*. Santa Fe, NM. Earthstar Press. 2003.

Starnes, Marian Young. *Letters from Summerland: A Bridge between the Worlds*. Cedar Mountain, NC. Terra Nova Publishing. 1996.

Whitehouse, Maggy. *Total Kabbalah: Bring Balance and Happiness into Your Life*. San Francisco, CA. Chronicle Books, LLC. 2008

Wolf, Rabbi Laibl. *Practical Kabbalah: A Guide to Jewish Wisdom for Everyday Life*. New York. Three Rivers Press. 1999.

ABOUT THE AUTHOR

For more than twenty-five years, Anne Hess practiced dental hygiene in North Carolina and Virginia. Working one-on-one with patients, Anne was committed to improving the quality of people's lives. But the crisis of her daughter's death in 2006 presented Anne with the greatest challenge of her life: learning how to recover from the pain of profound grief. Through all the stages of her own healing experience, Anne has developed a deep understanding and compassion for those who suffer the death of a loved one.

The focus of her life has now expanded, and it is her greatest hope that her story will help many others to navigate through their pain and find a new life of joy, love, and service to others. Anne Hess lives in Raleigh, North Carolina, and can be reached at www.thestrayawaychild.com.